How We Comm

Written by Lin Picou

Rourke
Educational Media

rourkeeducationalmedia.com

Scan for Related Titles
and Teacher Resources

www.rourkeeducationalmedia.com

PHOTO CREDITS: Cover & title page; © Mark Bowden, © PonyWang: © Quan Yin ; page 4: © Kouptsova; page 5: Monkey Business Images; page 6: © aabejon; page 7: © Wicki58; page 8: © asiseeit; page 9:© iofoto; page 10: © Konstantin Sutyagin, © Kyolshin; page 11: © Photoeuphoria; page 13: © Tiya; page 14: © Joshua Minso; page 15: © Orhan Çam, © Scol22; page 16: © Ruth Black; page 17: © Digital Storm; page 18: © innovatedcaptures; page 19: © nano; page 20: © Wavebreakmedia Ltd; page 21

Edited by: Jill Sherman

Cover: Tara Raymo

Interior design by: Pam McCollum

Library of Congress PCN Data

How We Communicate / Lin Picou
(Little World Social Studies)
ISBN 978-1-62169-916-3 (hard cover)(alk. paper)
ISBN 978-1-62169-811-1(soft cover)
ISBN 978-1-62717-021-5 (e-Book)
Library of Congress Control Number: 2013937310

Also Available as:

ROURKE'S
e-Books

Rourke Educational Media
Printed in the United States of America,
North Mankato, Minnesota

Rourke
Educational Media

rourkeeducationalmedia.com

customerservice@rourkeeducationalmedia.com • PO Box 643328 Vero Beach, Florida 32964

Table of Contents

Let's Talk

Waah! The baby cries to tell his mother he wants something right away.

Good manners are always important when talking to people. Listen and be polite.

You don't have to cry to get what you want because you know how to communicate with words. You use **verbal** and **nonverbal** communication.

Speaking is verbal communication.

Nonverbal communication is often silent.

When you communicate verbally, you talk to give information.

You might have a **conversation** about your day with your family during dinner.

When others are talking, be polite and wait your turn. Or, say "Excuse me" if you would like to talk.

A friend may call you on the phone to ask about homework.

If you and your grandmother have webcams on your **computers**, you could use your webcam to sing to her. Whenever you talk, you use verbal communication.

Without Words

Some information is communicated without talking. This is nonverbal communication.

When you are on the Internet, you are not speaking to anyone, but you must be careful. Some websites are not for children. You should always ask your parents or teachers for permission.

Your mother might write a note, or e-mail your teacher, if you miss school.

Dear Mrs. Robins,

Please excuse Evan from school last week.

Evan was sick with the flu.

Kind Regards,

Patricia Smith

You might write a book report to tell about what you read.

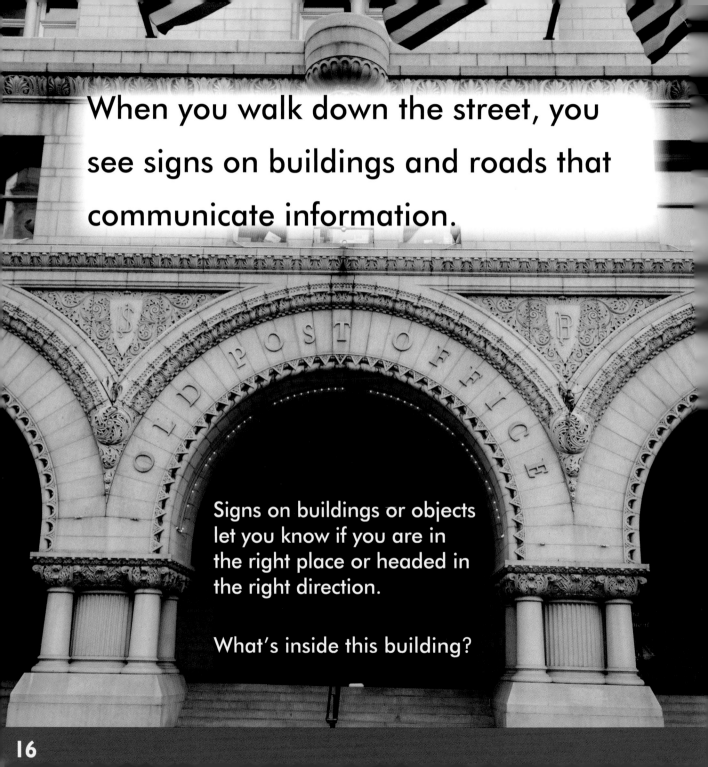

When you walk down the street, you see signs on buildings and roads that communicate information.

Signs on buildings or objects let you know if you are in the right place or headed in the right direction.

What's inside this building?

If you get a party **invitation** in the mail, it communicates the time and place of the celebration.

Hey Sweetie!
You're invited to
a Valentine's Day Party!
When: Saturday, February 14
at 1:00 p.m.
Where: Lauren's House
321 Sunnybrook Lane

What other communication can you find in your mailbox?

People can also communicate without talking or writing.

When you see the lights and hear the sirens of an emergency vehicle you know to pull your car to the side of the road.

A referee blows his whistle and uses his hands as signals to communicate to the players during a game. Touchdown!

You use **body language** when you raise your hand with a question for your teacher, or when you look at her to show you are listening.

What are you communicating when you clap? Smile? Give a thumbs up? A high-five?

There is so much information communicated every day. Now that you have learned about communication, you are ready to jump right in!

Picture Glossary

 **body language** (BOD-ee LANG-gwij): You can get clues to what a person is thinking by his gestures, postures, or facial expressions.

 **computers** (kuhm-PYOO-tuhrz): Electronic machines that can store, recall, or process information.

 **conversation** (kon-ver-SAY-shuhn): A conversation is when we exchange thoughts or ideas by talking.

invitation (in-vi-TAY-shuhn): A verbal or nonverbal request to come to an event or activity.

nonverbal (NON-vur-buhl): When you communicate without using your voice or speaking.

verbal (VUR-buhl): When you speak or communicate with your voice using spoken words.

Index

Websites

www.kidscommunicating.org/medialiteracy.html

www.kidcourses.com/sign-language-asl

www.kidscommunicating.org/links-to-great-speeches.html

About the Author

Lin Picou earned her Master's Degree in Language Arts at the University of South Florida. She teaches her students about all types of communication during her Pre-K class. Mrs. Picou's favorite forms of communication are books and the signs she sees while traveling. She loves to read about faraway places, then visit them.

Meet The Author!
www.meetREMauthors.com